W9-BKV-771

DISCARD

Published by Creative Education
P.O. Box 227, Mankato, Minnesota 56002
Creative Education is an imprint of The Creative Company

Design by Stephanie Blumenthal; Production by The Design Lab
Printed in the United States of America

Photographs by KAC Productions (Kathy Adams Clark, Larry Ditto, Peter
Gottschling, Glen Hayes, Greg Lasley, John & Gloria Tveten)

Library of Congress Cataloging-in-Publication Data
Frisch, Aaron.
Prairies / by Aaron Frisch.
p. cm. — (Our world)
Includes index.
ISBN 978-1-58341-572-6
1. Prairie ecology—Juvenile literature. 2. Prairies—Juvenile literature. I. Title
QH541.5.P7F75 2008   577.4'4—dc22   2006102990

First edition
2 4 6 8 9 7 5 3 1

OUR WORLD

PRAIRIES

Aaron Frisch

Prairies are big areas with lots of grass. Sometimes prairies are called "grass-lands." There are prairies all over the world. There is a big prairie in the middle of the United States. It is called the "Great Plains."

There are lots of different kinds of grass on prairies. Buffalo grass is a kind of grass that is short. Big bluestem is a kind of grass that is tall. Most grass on a prairie is green or yellow.

Many prairies look green or yellow

Most prairies do not have many trees. But prairies have small plants called shrubs and forbs. Shrubs are like little trees. Forbs are plants that die in the winter.

*Most prairie plants
do not grow tall*

Prairies have good soil. Soil is the dirt the grass grows from. Most land used by farmers used to be prairie. The farmers plant **crops** where prairie grass used to be. The good soil helps the crops grow.

There are lots of farms on prairies

Prairies can be cold or hot

Most prairies are far away from oceans. Many prairies are hot in the summer. Some prairies are very cold in the winter. There can be big storms on prairies.

Many animals find food on the prairie

Lots of animals live on prairies. There used to be lots of **bison** on the Great Plains. Bison are sometimes called buffalo. People killed almost all of the bison. But some bison still live on prairies today.

There are lots of **prong-horn** and prairie dogs on prairies. Snakes and coyotes *(ky-OH-teez)* live on prairies, too. So do birds like wild turkeys. Bugs like grasshoppers live there, too. In Africa, there are prairies that have lions and zebras.

Pronghorn live by snakes and turkeys

Prairies can be hurt. Farm cows can hurt prairies if they eat too much grass. Farmers can hurt prairies by **plowing** the ground to plant crops. When the ground gets plowed too often, the wind can blow away the soil. This turns the prairie into a **desert**.

Some prairies turn into deserts

Prairies are special places. Lots of animals and plants live there. Farmers need the good soil that comes from prairies. And prairies are pretty to look at!

Prairies have lots of flowers and bugs

The grass on a prairie has roots. Roots are like fingers that help hold on to the soil. Almost all plants have roots. You can see how roots hold on to soil. Find a plant that has been growing in a pot for a while (ask your parents if it is okay first). Pull the plant out of the dirt. See how the roots hold on to the soil?

GLOSSARY

bison—big animals that have horns and thick fur

crops—the plants that a farmer grows

desert—a dry area with lots of sand

plowing—digging up dirt or soil to plant things in it

pronghorn—an animal like a deer; it has small horns and runs very fast

LEARN MORE ABOUT PRAIRIES

Enchanted Learning
http://www.enchantedlearning.com/biomes/grassland/prairie.shtml
This site has lots of pictures of prairie animals.

Missouri Botanical Garden
http://www.mbgnet.net/sets/grasslnd/index.htm
This site has all kinds of facts about prairies.